Forget Me Not:

Armenian Genocide Recollections

Ariana Kabodian

Ariana Kabodian (signature)

Thank you for your
interest in Armenian history.
Peace & Love

Ariana Kabodian (signature)

Chapbook Press

Schuler Books
2660 28th Street SE
Grand Rapids, MI 49512
(616) 942-7330
www.schulerbooks.com

Forget Me Not: Armenian Genocide Recollections

ISBN 13: 9781948237710

Library of Congress Control Number: 2021903750

Printed in the United States by Chapbook Press.

This book is dedicated to all Armenians, and to my ancestors who survived the Armenian Genocide.

Their perseverance and survival provided the path for my life and my ability to write this book, which is an honor.

May their lives and sacrifice never be forgotten.

This book is also dedicated to my parents, thank you for everything.

Acknowledgements

To my family, thank you for willing to share our history and photographs. I am so grateful for your support and love.

Anne Marie (Zallakian) Ameriguian, M.D.
Shoushan "Susan (Artar) Ameriguian
Mary Ann (Karakashian) Artinian
Adam Asadoorian
Alice (Kabodian) Asadoorian
Judge Lisa L. Asadoorian
Ara Barsoumian
Brenda (Markarian) Barsoumian
Mary (Shirozian) Hatzakorzian
Cathy (Masropian) Hendel
Laurie (Kabodian) Jackson
Aram Kabodian
Armen Kabodian
Belinda (Ameriguian) Kabodian
Margaux Kabodian
Nazeli "Hazel" Kabodian
Sally (Godoshian) Kabodian
Samson Shun Kabodian
Denise (Dourjalian) Karakashian
Jack Karakashian
Robert "Bobby" Karakashian
Anahid (Zallakian) Kazanjian
Denise (Masropian) King
Briske (Terzian) Mampourian
Yester (Terzian) Manankichian
Aghavni "Agnes" (Klavanian) Markarian
Andrew Markarian
Ani Markarian
Edward "Eddie" Markarian
Linda Markarian
Silva (Artar) Markarian
Tamara (Kabodian) Markarian
Taleen Markarian
Thomas "Tommy" Markarian
Meliné Nichols
Robert Nichols
Sona (Artar) Nichols
James Patterson
Hampartsoum "Hampy" Terzian
Barbara (Dourjalian) Widener
Alice (Soultanian) Zallakian
Michael "Raffi" Zallakian

A Hope Unspoken
~ Aram Kabodian

Sometimes I forget

they lived with the pain of their parents' murders
no safety net, no example, no peace
life was of their making
with a daily pain remembered

Sometimes I forget

they were so young and came so far
it could have been any place
but they settled here
led to this more perfect place

Sometimes I forget

they spoke from their hearts
but were not understood
for their words were foreign
this new land distrustful

Sometimes I forget

they coped with little
provided for many
complained minimally
praised the Lord

They laughed, sang, danced, hugged
life
with a hope unspoken:
my life.

Table of Contents

Prologue

This book contains stories of events and experiences from survivors of the Armenian Genocide and the Istanbul Pogrom. Every recollection within this book is from a direct or indirect family member of the author, Ariana Kabodian, who is 100% Armenian. This book was written to convey the events in the Armenian Genocide and Istanbul Pogrom, preserve her family's history, and spread awareness about Armenia. In case you are unfamiliar with Armenia, here is some information about the country and culture.

Armenia is home to about 3 million Armenians and is near the Mediterranean Sea in West Asia.[1] Armenia was the first nation to declare Christianity as its official religion in 301 AD.[2] Traditional Armenian food includes choreg bread, rice pilaf, kabobs, spinach beoreg, and wrapped grape leaves, known as sarma. In Armenia, tourism attractions include the Cafesjian Center for the Arts, Mt. Ararat, Lake Sevan, The Etchmiadzin Cathedral, and the Armenian Genocide Memorial.[3] The national fruits of Armenia are apricots and pomegranates.[4]

---

[1] Wilson, Joshn. Jonathan Rainey. GeoHistory: Armenia Armenia: a Global People. 24 November 2015. https://geohistory.today/armenia/
[2] HEARING BEFORE THE COMMISSION ON SECURITY AND COOPERATION IN EUROPE ONE HUNDRED FOURTEENTH CONGRESS FIRST SESSION. *A CENTURY OF DENIAL: THE ARMENIAN GENOCIDE AND THE ONGOING QUEST FOR JUSTICE.* APRIL 23, 2015. U.S. GOVERNMENT PUBLISHING OFFICE: Washington 2015. p 52. https://www.govinfo.gov/content/pkg/CHRG-114jhrg95113/pdf/CHRG-114jhrg95113.pdf
[3] Trip.com. *Top Things to Do in Armenia in 2020.* Retrieved on 12.29.2020. https://www.trip.com/travel-guide/armenia-20372/tourist-attractions/
[4] Armenia Discovery. *Armenian Fruits.* 16 April 2019. Accessed on 1.1.2021. Retrieved from: https://armeniadiscovery.com/en/articles/armenian-fruits#:~:text=Armenian%20fruit%20%231%20Apricot,apricots%20were%20originated%20from%20Armenia

The History of the Armenian Genocide

The Armenian Genocide of 1.5 million innocent Armenians was carried out by the Ottoman Empire (modern-day Turkey) from 1915-1923.[5] The Armenian Genocide was the first modern Genocide.[6] The purpose of the Armenian Genocide was to annihilate Armenians.[7] Genocide is an internationally recognized crime that occurs with the intent to destroy an entire group.[8] Genocide also refers to the murder of a whole nation.[9] The Hamidian Massacres, also known as the Armenian Massacres, occurred from 1894-1896.[10] During that time, the Ottoman Empire killed 300,000 Armenians, and was the foreshadowing event of the Armenian Genocide.[11]

The Armenian Genocide began with the Shabin-Karahisar uprising in Sebinkarahisar, Turkey, from June 2nd – June 30th, 1915.[12] During that month, Armenians held back the Ottoman troops at The Castle at Sebinkarahisar until they were overtaken and everyone in the entire city was massacred.[13]

During the Armenian Genocide, Armenian males were killed first. The Turkish soldiers had a priority list on who to kill afterward;

[5] United States Holocaust Memorial Museum. *"The Armenian Genocide: In Depth."* Holocaust Encyclopedia. Accessed on 12.29.2020. Retrieved from: https://encyclopedia.ushmm.org/content/en/article/introduction-to-the-holocaust
[6] Dawoodi, DJ. Sociology and Criminology-Open Access. *The Aftermath of the Armenian Genocide and the Holocaust: A Comparative Study.* 18 December 2018. Department of History, University of Garmian, Kalar, Kurdistan, Iraq. Accessed on 12.29.2020. Retrieved from: https://www.longdom.org/open-access/the-aftermath-of-the-armenian-genocide-and-the-holocaust-a-comparative-study-2375-4435-1000183.pdf
[7] United States Holocaust Memorial Museum. *"The Armenian Genocide: In Depth."* Holocaust Encyclopedia. Accessed on 12.29.2020. Retrieved from: https://encyclopedia.ushmm.org/content/en/article/introduction-to-the-holocaust
[8] What is Genocide? *United States Holocaust Memorial Museum.* Accessed on 12.30.2020. Retrieved from: https://www.ushmm.org/genocide-prevention/learn-about-genocide-and-other-mass-atrocities/what-is-genocide
[9] Cambridge Dictionary. Genocide. Accessed on 12.29.2020. Retrieved from: https://dictionary.cambridge.org/us/dictionary/english/genocide 12.30.2020
[10] Cohan, Sara. *A Brief History of the Armenian Genocide.* Social Education 69(6), pg. 335. ©2005 National Council for the Social Studies. Accessed on 1.11.2021. Retrieved from: http://www.ignaciodarnaude.com/espiritualismo/Armenian%20genocide,Brief%20history.pdf
[11] Cohan, Sara. *A Brief History of the Armenian Genocide.* Social Education 69(6), pg. 335. ©2005 National Council for the Social Studies. Accessed on 1.11.2021. Retrieved from: http://www.ignaciodarnaude.com/espiritualismo/Armenian%20genocide,Brief%20history.pdf
[12] *Shabin-Karahisar Uprising.* Compiled by World Heritage Encyclopedia™. Accessed on 12.29.2020. Retrieved from: http://community.worldheritage.org/articles/eng/Shabin-Karahisar_uprising
[13] *Shabin-Karahisar Uprising.* Compiled by World Heritage Encyclopedia™. Accessed on 12.29.2020. Retrieved from: http://community.worldheritage.org/articles/eng/Shabin-Karahisar_uprising

and it began with those with honorable professions and higher class, and then they killed their way down the ranks.[14] Armenian elders, women, and children were deported, raped, and or forced to go on death marches through The Syrian Desert to a concentration camp named Deir ez-Zor, located in the middle of the desert.[15]

Those who survived the Armenian Genocide were dispersed throughout the world;[16] and many migrated to The United States, where their descendants primarily reside in Los Angles, Detroit, Boston, and Philadelphia.[17]

Many years later, terror again struck Armenians with the Istanbul Pogrom on September 6th, 1955, when Turkey attacked Armenians and Grecians.[18] Pogrom is an act of cruelty or killing done to many people because of their race or religion.[19] During this time, hundreds of Armenians and Grecians were robbed, attacked, killed, and raped; many homes and Orthodox Churches were burned and destroyed.[20] There is no official Turkish police report that this occurred.[21]

Turkey denies the Armenian Genocide occurred and refuses to take responsibility, which is why it is also referred to as the

---

[14] Theriault, Henry C. *Genocide, Denial, and Domination: Armenian-Turkish Relations from Conflict Resolution to Just Transformation.* 2009 Sept. Journal of African Conflicts and Peace Studies. Volume 1: Issue 2 Genocide: Critical Issues. P.83-90. Accessed on 12.29.20. Retrieved from: https://scholarcommons.usf.edu/cgi/viewcontent.cgi?article=1019&context=jacaps
[15] Theriault, Henry C. *Genocide, Denial, and Domination: Armenian-Turkish Relations from Conflict Resolution to Just Transformation.* 2009 Sept. Journal of African Conflicts and Peace Studies. Volume 1: Issue 2 Genocide: Critical Issues. P.83-90. Accessed on 12.29.20. Retrieved from: https://scholarcommons.usf.edu/cgi/viewcontent.cgi?article=1019&context=jacaps
[16] Encyclopedia Entries on the Armenian Genocide: *Armenian Genocide (1915-1923).* Accessed on 12.29.2020. Retrieved from: https://www.armenian-genocide.org/genocide.html
[17] Kiprop, Victor. 23 September 2019. Society. World Atlas. *States with the Largest Populations of Armenian Americans.* Accessed on 12.29.2020. Retrieved from: https://www.worldatlas.com/articles/states-with-the-largest-populations-of-armenian-americans.html
[18] De Zayas, Alfred. The Istanbul Pogrom of 6–7 September 1955 in the Light of International Law. August 2007. Volume 2, Issue 2. *Genocide Studies and Prevention: An International Journal.* Accessed on 12.29.20. Retrieved from: https://scholarcommons.usf.edu/cgi/viewcontent.cgi?article=1206&context=gsp
[19] Cambridge Dictionary. Pogrom. Accessed on 1.1.2021. Retrieved from: https://dictionary.cambridge.org/us/dictionary/english/pogrom
[20] De Zayas, Alfred. The Istanbul Pogrom of 6–7 September 1955 in the Light of International Law. August 2007. Volume 2, Issue 2. *Genocide Studies and Prevention: An International Journal.* Accessed on 12.29.20. Retrieved from: https://scholarcommons.usf.edu/cgi/viewcontent.cgi?article=1206&context=gsp
[21] De Zayas, Alfred. The Istanbul Pogrom of 6–7 September 1955 in the Light of International Law. August 2007. Volume 2, Issue 2. P.138. *Genocide Studies and Prevention: An International Journal.* Accessed on 12.29.2020. Retrieved from: https://scholarcommons.usf.edu/cgi/viewcontent.cgi?article=1206&context=gsp

Forgotten Genocide.[22] The remembrance of the Armenian Genocide is recognized annually on April 24th. Thirty countries recognize the Armenian Genocide,[23] including The United States.[24] In 2019, The United States Congress officially recognized the Armenian Genocide and mandated that it be included in history courses.

[25]

Crosses shown at St. John's Armenian Church in Michigan represent the 1.5 million Armenians killed during the Armenian Genocide

[22] Theriault, Henry C. *Genocide, Denial, and Domination: Armenian-Turkish Relations from Conflict Resolution to Just Transformation.* 2009 Sept. Journal of African Conflicts and Peace Studies. Volume 1: Issue 2 Genocide: Critical Issues. P.86. Accessed on 12.29.2020. Retrieved from: https://scholarcommons.usf.edu/cgi/viewcontent.cgi?article=1019&context=jacaps
[23] Armenian National Institute. *Countries that Recognize the Armenian Genocide.* Accessed on 12.29.2020. Retrieved from: https://www.armenian-genocide.org/recognition_countries.html
[24] United States Senate Committee on Foreign Relations.12 December 2019. Senate Passes Menendez Resolution Recognizing the Armenian Genocide. https://www.foreign.senate.gov/press/ranking/release/senate-passes-menendez-resolution-recognizing-the-armenian-genocide
[25] Image provided by Ariana Kabodian

Armenian Genocide Recollections

Meliné (Dilan) Artar

Meliné (Dilan) Artar's life was shared by her daughters, Shoushan "Susan" (Artar) Ameriguian and Silva (Artar) Markarian. Meliné was born in 1914, in Gumushacikoy, Turkey, to the parents of Imasdum (Baravarian) Dilanian and Vahan Dilanian. They owned a company that provided the means for many occupations, including shoemakers, wool importers, clothing makers, and merchants. Vahan and Imasdum wanted many children so that they could carry on the family business, and had seven children, with Meliné being the youngest. The family came from enormous wealth, and lived on a 10 acre mansion that had an art gallery, pool, library, an apple orchard, and a water fountain in their courtyard. Her family lived a happy life until the Armenian Genocide.

Meliné was only a few months old when her Father, Grandfather, and her Uncle, Garabed Artar, were murdered by Turkish soldiers. They also took the men's wealth, art, and money. Thankfully, Imasdum was independently wealthy, but was left to raise seven children on her own. Vahan's sister, Mariam (Dilanian) Artar, had no wealth, and had to raise her five children; two of whom died in the Genocide. Imasdum graciously took in Mariam and her three children, and they all lived together until Meliné was 18. Due to the constant threat Armenians faced as a result of the Genocide, the family chose to remove the common Armenian last-name signature of "ian" from Dilanian, and changed their last name to Dilan, in order to conceal their identity.

Due to the killings of the Genocide, Imasdum and Mariam were desperate to keep the next generation in their family Armenian. Unfortunately, they had no other option but to arrange for their children to marry. In 1932, and at the age of 18, Meliné married her cousin, Mesiya Artar in Gumushacikoy, Turkey. They had three daughters: Shoushan "Susan" (Artar) Ameriguian, the eldest, was born in 1934, and Silva (Artar) Markarian was born in 1936. Mesiya was an electrician and mechanic, and Meliné was an excellent Armenian cook; and together they raised their daughters. Mesiya was so handy that in 1937, a hurricane destroyed their house, and he rebuilt the family's home.

A few years later, the family moved to Istanbul, Turkey, where their youngest daughter, Sona (Artar) Nichols, was born in 1949. While living in Istanbul, the girls attended The Getronagan Lisa Academy in Karakoy, Turkey because education was a priority.

They lived in Istanbul until the Istanbul Pogrom occurred in 1955. Soon after, the Artar Family decided it was time to immigrate to The United States for a safer life. Shoushan immigrated first in 1957 and went to Detroit, Michigan. Silva immigrated with her husband, Toros "Tony" Markarian, to Boston, Massachusetts, in 1962. Soon after, Sona followed Silva, and joined her sister in Boston in 1964. Meliné immigrated to Boston shortly after in 1966, and then brought Mesiya to Boston in 1969.

Meliné and Mesiya were happily married for 49 years until Mesiya passed away in 1982. Many years later, Meliné peacefully passed away in Boston in 2005. She was one of the last living survivors of the Armenian Genocide and she passed away at the age of 91 in 2005. Her daughters remember her as someone loved deeply and enjoyed life; she was one of the nicest people and always had a smile on her face.

Her granddaughter, Belinda (Ameriguian) Kabodian, spoke fondly of her Grandmother who she called Medzmama (Armenian word for Grandmother). Every summer when Belinda was a child, she would stay with her Medzmama in Boston. She loved being with her and watching her cook and bake Armenian dishes, and she was a loving influence in her life.

⌃Back from left: Mesiya Artar, Araxie (Dilan) Tascioglu, & Antranig Tascioglu

Front from left: Shoushan (Artar) Ameriguian, Imasdum (Baravarian) Dilan & Nurhan Tascioglu

⌃ Back from left: Azniv Dilan, (the maid, Lusapen,), & Haygouhi Dilan (Meliné (Dilan) Artar's sisters)

Front from left: Khachig Baravarian, Zarouhi Baravarian, Imasdum (Baravarian) Dilan, & Vahan Dilan

---

[26] Image provided by Shoushan (Artar) Ameriguia
[27] Image provided by Brenda (Markarian) Barsoumian

Shoushan "Susan" (Artar) Ameriguian

Shoushan "Susan" (Artar) Ameriguian was born on October 29th, 1934 to Meliné (Dilan) Artar and Mesiya Artar in Gumushacikoy, Turkey. She is the eldest to her two younger sisters, Silva (Artar) Markarian and Sona (Artar) Nichols.

Her Father, Mesiya, was an electrician and mechanic, and her Mother, Meliné, was an excellent cook. Some of Shoushan's favorite memories of her Mother was her Armenian dishes such as tertipaz, kourabia, and her orange zest cookies are a family favorite.

Shoushan and Silva became teachers, and Shoushan recalled the beginning of the Istanbul Pogrom. She recalls her and Silva walking home from teaching on September 7th, 1955, and seeing the Turkish soldiers causing havoc on Armenians and Grecians. Shoushan recalled being fearful for her and her sister's lives because the soldiers were burning Armenian Orthodox Churches, stealing, attacking, and killing people. She remembers approaching their home and her Mother being overcome in grief, thinking her daughters were killed in the attacks. The Istanbul Pogrom lasted for days; it was during that time that Shoushan decided she would immigrate to The United States for a safer life.

Shoushan's Aunt, Haygouhi Solakian, helped Shoushan obtain a visa to travel to The United States. On March 31st, 1957, at the age of 23, she arrived in New York with no money or belongings. She stayed at her Aunt's house for a few days, and then shortly after arrival, had an arranged marriage to Joseph Ameriguian who was an Armenian immigrant from Marseille, France. She recalled how they went on a few dates, and then married on June 8th, 1957. Afterwards, then lived in Detroit for a few years while Joseph worked at the Ford Motor Company.

Shoushan and Joseph welcomed their first son in 1958 and bought a home in 1960 in Detroit. Shoushan is a talented seamstress; she had a career working for Hudson's, Marshall Fields, and Macys. While they were living in Detroit, they had another child in 1960, Brian, who unfortunately died soon after birth. A few years later, they had a daughter, Belinda (Ameriguian) Kabodian in 1963, and moved to Dearborn in 1968, where they resided until Joseph's passing in 1985.

Shoushan moved to Novi, Michigan after Joseph's passing, and lives there and in Delray Beach, Florida. She enjoys being a Grandmother to her four grandchildren as well as being an active member of the Women's Guild at St. John's Armenian Church. She is a proud Bolsetsee, which means she is an Armenian from Istanbul. She is a talented cook and baker and creates delicious Armenian meals. She lived a very stressful and challenging life, with many obstacles which she overcame. Shoushan is thankful she decided to immigrate to The United States.

《 Back from left: Shoushan (Artar) Ameriguian, Meliné (Dilan) Artar, Mesiya Artar & Silva (Artar) Markarian

Front: Sona (Artar) Nichols

Shoushan (Artar) 》 Ameriguian

《 From Left: Shoushan (Artar) Ameriguian & Joseph Ameriguian

---

[28] Image provided by Shoushan (Artar) Ameriguian
[29] Image Provided by Belinda (Ameriguian) Kabodian
[30] Image provided by Shoushan (Artar) Ameriguian

Ramela (Nushanian) Carman

Ramela (Nushanian) Carman was born on April 7th, 1914, to Mihran and Makroui Nushanian in Yozgat, Turkey.[31] Before to the Armenian Genocide, her Father was a tradesman who provided a very comfortable life for her family. Unfortunately, he died in 1919 from kidney problems, and shortly after, Ramela's infant brother died from cholera.

Ramela carried the memories of escaping the Genocide with her throughout her life. During the escape, she suffered a facial injury; and a Turkish woman took her and her Mother in and helped her recover.[32] To protect Ramela from the Genocide, Makroui took Ramela and her Mother to live in Istanbul, Turkey, where Makroui worked in a factory.[33] When Ramela was 16, she became the sole provider for her family and worked in a factory sewing shirts.[34] She immigrated to The United States in 1960 and married Masa Carman shortly after arriving.[35] She taught herself how to speak English and was hired by Hagopian World of Rugs and repaired oriental rugs.[36] While Ramela and Masa lived in Dearborn Heights, she befriended her neighbor, Shoushan (Artar) Ameriguian who

---

[31] Runkle, Anne. The Oakland Press. *Ramela Carman, one of world's last survivors of Armenian Genocide, dies at 102.* August 8, 2016. Accessed on 1.3.2021. Retrieved from: https://www.theoaklandpress.com/news/nation-world-news/ramela-carman-one-of-world-s-last-survivors-of-armenian-genocide-dies-at-102/article_0d0bfeea-9595-5519-8a8f-7f3e01401ec0.html

[32] Warikoo, Niraj. *Detroit Free Press. Michigan's last survivor of Armenian genocide dies at 102.* August 8 2016. Accessed on 1.3.2021. Retrieved from: https://www.freep.com/story/news/obituary/2016/08/09/armenian-massacre-survivor-ramela-carman/88463482/

[33] Runkle, Anne. The Oakland Press. *Ramela Carman, one of world's last survivors of Armenian Genocide, dies at 102.* August 8, 2016. Accessed on 1.3.2021. Retrieved from: https://www.theoaklandpress.com/news/nation-world-news/ramela-carman-one-of-world-s-last-survivors-of-armenian-genocide-dies-at-102/article_0d0bfeea-9595-5519-8a8f-7f3e01401ec0.html

[34] Runkle, Anne. The Oakland Press. *Ramela Carman, one of world's last survivors of Armenian Genocide, dies at 102.* August 8, 2016. Accessed on 1.3.2021. Retrieved from: https://www.theoaklandpress.com/news/nation-world-news/ramela-carman-one-of-world-s-last-survivors-of-armenian-genocide-dies-at-102/article_0d0bfeea-9595-5519-8a8f-7f3e01401ec0.html

[35] Runkle, Anne. The Oakland Press. *Ramela Carman, one of world's last survivors of Armenian Genocide, dies at 102.* August 8, 2016. Accessed on 1.3.2021. Retrieved from: https://www.theoaklandpress.com/news/nation-world-news/ramela-carman-one-of-world-s-last-survivors-of-armenian-genocide-dies-at-102/article_0d0bfeea-9595-5519-8a8f-7f3e01401ec0.html

[36] Runkle, Anne. The Oakland Press. *Ramela Carman, one of world's last survivors of Armenian Genocide, dies at 102.* August 8, 2016. Accessed on 1.3.2021. Retrieved from: https://www.theoaklandpress.com/news/nation-world-news/ramela-carman-one-of-world-s-last-survivors-of-armenian-genocide-dies-at-102/article_0d0bfeea-9595-5519-8a8f-7f3e01401ec0.html

retold her story. They became great friends, and were neighbors for almost 30 years. Shoushan recalled that Ramela was a very happy person, despite having lived through the Genocide. She also loved being a member of St. John's Armenian Church. Shoushan carries Ramela's memory with her daily.

Ramela passed away on August 6th, 2016, at the age of 102; she was blessed to be married to Masa, and they lived a happy life together. Ramela (Nushanian) Carman was the last living Armenian Genocide survivor in Michigan,[37] and one of the last survivors in the world.[38]

[39]

Ramela (Nushanian) Carman

[37] Warikoo, Niraj. *Detroit Free Press. Michigan's last survivor of Armenian genocide dies at 102.* August 8 2016. Accessed on 1.3.2021. Retrieved from: https://www.freep.com/story/news/obituary/2016/08/09/armenian-massacre-survivor-ramela-carman/88463482/
[38] Runkle, Anne. The Oakland Press. *Ramela Carman, one of world's last survivors of Armenian Genocide, dies at 102.* August 8, 2016. Accessed on 1.3.2021. Retrieved from: https://www.theoaklandpress.com/news/nation-world-news/ramela-carman-one-of-world-s-last-survivors-of-armenian-genocide-dies-at-102/article_0d0bfeea-9595-5519-8a8f-7f3e01401ec0.html
[39] Runkle, Anne. The Oakland Press. *Ramela Carman, one of world's last survivors of Armenian Genocide, dies at 102.* August 8, 2016. Accessed on 1.3.2021. Retrieved from: https://www.theoaklandpress.com/news/nation-world-news/ramela-carman-one-of-world-s-last-survivors-of-armenian-genocide-dies-at-102/article_0d0bfeea-9595-5519-8a8f-7f3e01401ec0.html

Manoug Markarian

Manoug Markarian's life was shared by his daughter in law, Silva (Artar) Markarian. Manoug was born in 1886, in Kayseri, Turkey. Because he tough life due to the Armenian Genocide, very little is known about his youth.

When Manoug was a young adult, he got married. His wife and five children resided in Armenia while Manoug worked in The United States, and he would send all his earnings to provide for his family. When the Genocide began in 1915, Turkish soldiers murdered Manoug's wife and five children. Manoug was devastated; even more so because he could not return to Armenia to give himself closure due to the threat Armenians faced of being killed upon arrival.

A few years later, he met his second wife, an Armenian named Siranoush, and they got married in Massachusetts in 1921. Their marriage was interesting at first because Manoug only spoke Armenian, and Siranoush only spoke Turkish. After some time, they eventually were able to translate and understand one another. They had four children: Lucy, twins Toros "Tony" and Elizabeth, and Michael. Manoug founded M&T Oil Company (Metro Energy) in 1929. Manoug and Siranoush lived a happy life together until Manoug passed away in 1958, and Siranoush passed away in 1973 in Boston, Massachusetts.

⌃From Left: Siranoush Markarian
& Manoug Markarian

⌃ Manoug Markarian

[40] Image provided by Brenda (Markarian) Barsoumian
[41] Image provided by Brenda (Markarian) Barsoumian

Silva (Artar) Markarian

Silva (Artar) Markarian was born in 1936 to Meliné (Dilan) Artar and Mesiya Artar in Gumushacikoy, Turkey. She is the middle daughter to her two sisters, Shoushan (Artar) Ameriguian and Sona (Artar) Nichols.

Silva and her sister Shoushan were teachers, and Silva recalled her and Shoushan walking home from teaching on September 7th, 1955, while the Turkish soldiers were causing havoc on Armenians and Grecians, later to be known as the Istanbul Pogrom. Silva recalled how living in Istanbul as an Armenian was tough; it was unsafe, and a threat to their existence because they were Armenian.

A few years later, in 1962, Manoug and Siranoush Markarian's son, Toros, went to vacation in Europe in the summer in hopes of finding a wife. He met Silva Artar thorough his brother in law, and they were married a month later in Istanbul, Turkey. Toros and Silva went to Boston, Massachusetts, and Silva learned English from friends and from listening to the radio. Toros and Silva had four children, Brenda (Markarian) Barsoumian, Edward "Eddie" Markarian, Thomas "Tommy" Markarian, and Linda Markarian, and eventually had seven grandchildren. As Silva reminisced about her life, she fondly explained that she thankful God sent Toros to her. They were happily married for 56 years until Toros passed away in January 2019.

Shortly after Silva immigrated to Boston, her younger sister, Sona, immigrated to The United States in 1964 from Istanbul, Turkey, and lived with Silva and Toros. In 1971, Sona married Robert "Bobby" Nichols, and they got married in 1971. Sona spent her entire career working for Delta Airlines as a flight attendant, and Robert was the Tight End for the Boston Patriots (New England Patriots). They had two children, Robert Nichols and Meliné Nichols, in Boston, and were happily married until Robert Nichols passed away in 2005.

Silva and Sona reside on the waterfront of the Boston Harbor with their families. They are thankful to have their families safely living in The United States.

42

From Left: Sisters Shoushan (Artar) Ameriguian, Silva (Artar) Markarian & Sona (Artar) Nichols

---

《 From Left:
Toros Markarian
& Silva (Artar)
Markarian

43

Back from left: 》

Silva (Artar)
Markarian, Sona
(Artar) Nichols,
& Shoushan
(Artar)
Ameriguian

Front: Meliné
(Dilan) Artar

44

《 From Left:
Robert "Bobby"
Nichols & Silva
(Artar) Nichols

45

43 Image provided by Shoushan (Artar) Ameriguian
44 Image provided by Shoushan (Artar) Ameriguian
45 Image provided by Belinda (Ameriguian) Kabodia

Missak Barsoumian and Levon Barsoumian

Missak Barsoumian and Levon Barsoumian's experience was retold by Ara Barsoumian, (Missak's grandson and Levon's son). Missak was born in Aintab, presently known as Gaziantep, Turkey, in 1879. Little is known about his youth, but he was in his mid-30's, and his son, Levon, born in 1909, was six, when the Armenian Genocide began.

Thankfully, Aintab was not as affected by the Genocide as other towns were. In 1911, Missak had moved his family to Aleppo, Syria, where he and his son, Levon, hid many Armenians who were fleeing their villages, needing refuge. Because the Turkish soldiers paid little attention to the youth, Levon would guide families to refuge, and Missak would orchestrate the plan for each family's escape.

Levon would take the family to the rooflines, where they would jump from roof to roof to avoid the Turkish soldiers in the streets, and then hide them in crawl spaces of specific houses. One of the crawl spaces belonged to a Turkish family who disapproved of the Genocide. They hid Armenians in their home while the Father was out fighting as one of the Turkish soldiers. The Turkish household was the last place soldiers would look to find Armenians.

Shortly after the Genocide, Missak passed away in 1934. Levon and his brother moved to Beirut, Lebanon, in 1938, where he met his wife, Anahid (Bedrosian) Barsoumian, and they got married in 1941.

Levon and Anahid had four children: Vera (Barsoumian) Iskenderian, Missak Barsoumian, Berj Barsoumian, and Ara Barsoumian. Levon became a Civil Engineer who worked on many buildings, including The Barsoum Building in Beirut. The results of his philanthropy live to date, and Levon passed away in 1986.

Ara Barsoumian moved to The United States in 1976, where he completed his higher education and married Brenda (Markarian) Barsoumian. He has made every effort to keep the traditions and teachings of his Father and Grandfather alive.

⋀ Anahid Barsoumian & Levon Barsoumian

⋀ The Barsoumian siblings:

Back from left: Nerses Barsoumian, Baghdassar Barsoumian, Hovhannes Barsoumian, Missak Barsoumian

Front from left: Horrum Barsoumian, Annik Barsoumian, Mariam Barsoumian & Varter Barsoumian

[46] Image provided by Ara Barsoumian
[47] Image provided by Ara Barsoumian

Krikor Shirozian

Krikor Shirozian's life was retold by his granddaughter, Ani Markarian. In 1988, Krikor was interviewed where he discussed his experience in a documented YouTube video titled: *Krikor and Verjin Shirozian*.[48]

Krikor Shirozian was born in 1908 in Malatia, Armenia and his Father died soon after he was born. All of his family's records were burned from the Armenian Genocide. He was an only child, and was seven years old at the beginning of the Genocide in 1915. Because he was so young, he did not remember his Father's name but knew his Mother's name was Mary.

At the age of seven, Krikor was sitting on his Mother's lap when the Turkish soldiers came to their village. His Mother and relatives hid from the soldiers for an entire day. When he woke up the next morning, they had all disappeared; only he and his Grandmother remained. Unsure what to do, they joined big groups of Armenians, and walked with them into the Syrian Desert.

They walked until they got to Deir ez-Zor, the concentration camp in the Syrian Desert.[49] A Turkish soldier asked his Grandmother if he could take Krikor; since she knew they were all going to be killed, she agreed to spare his life. The Turkish soldier took him home, but his wife was abusive, and she would beat him.

---

[48] Shirozian, Sev. *Kirkor and Verjin Shirozian.* Recorded on April 9th, 1988. Posted on YouTube on August 2, 2015. Accessed on 1.12.2021. Retrieved from: https://www.youtube.com/watch?v=jEH8ZOnl-mc
[49] Mouradian, Khatchig. *Genocide and Humanitarian Resistance in Ottoman Syria, 1915-1916.* Open Edition Journals. p. 88. Accessed on 1.12.2021. Retrieved from: https://journals.openedition.org/eac/1023

When the soldier saw the bruises, he sold Krikor to another Turkish family.

From the ages of 15-16, Krikor was sold to many families and moved from one city to another. One night, he escaped, and eventually met someone in another village, who helped him get to Syria, where Armenians were safe.

Once he arrived in Syria, he was directed to go to an orphanage where he was given clothes and food. He attended school and learned Armenian. Once he finished school, he made a living working for a rug company.

While living in Syria, Armenian refuges recognized him, and were able to provide him with some family photos they saved; it was then he learned his last name, Shirozian.

In 1936, Krikor met his wife, Verjin, and at the age of 28 in Aleppo, Syria, they married, and eventually had four children. Mary (Shirozian) Hatzakorzian, one of Krikor and Verjin's children was named after Krikor's Mother, Mary.

In 1973, Krikor and his entire family (including Mary (Shirozian) Hatzakorzian and Mary's daughter, Ani Markarian), immigrated to Philadelphia, Pennsylvania. Krikor loved living in Philadelphia, and lived the rest of his life peacefully with his family. He loved gardening and enjoyed growing fruits and vegetables.

Krikor Shirozian passed away in Philadelphia at the age of 86 in 1995. Krikor's childhood never left him, and whenever he would talk about it, he would always cry.

(Left) young adult & (Right) adult Krikor Shirozian

Mardiros Godoshian

Mardiros Godoshian was born to Nishon Godoshian and Sima (Mikaelian) Godoshian, and grew up in Gavar, "Garva" Armenia. Before the Armenian Genocide, Nishon temporarily moved to The United States to help provide for his family. When the Genocide began in 1915 and Mardiros was eight years old, his Mother and sister were murdered; only he was spared.

Mardiros then wandered throughout Turkey and Syria, trying to locate any surviving relatives. Mardiros ended up years later at The Anteb Orphanage in Turkey, where he was reunited with his Father. Mardiros, at the age of 14, arrived in The United States with his Father in Pontiac, Michigan, where they lived and worked.

Several years later, at the age of 21, Mardiros met his wife, Kagazig (Kurkjian), and married in 1925. He worked at The Wilson Foundry Machine Shop and for The Stanley Berry Door Company and owned his own lawn care business. They were happily marriage and had four children: Sema (Godoshian) Dakesian, twins Sally (Godoshian) Kabodian and Sirouhi (Godoshian) Kemsuzian, and Michael Godoshian. They were married for 61 years and had a wonderful life until Mardiros died in 1986.

Sally (Godoshian) Kabodian, who shared her Father's life, remembered him as a hard-working, happy man with a great sense of humor, and who was very devoted to his family.

⌃ From Left: Mardiros Godoshian
& Kagazig (Kurkjian) Godoshian

⌃ Back from left: Sirouhi (Godoshian) Kemsuzian, Sema
(Godoshian) Dakesian & Sally (Godoshian) Kabodian

Front from left: Mardiros Godoshian, &
Kagazig (Kurkjian) Godoshian

Kagazig (Kurkjian) Godoshian

Kagazig (Kurkjian) Godoshian was born in Tripoli, Turkey in 1902. She was the youngest daughter and was one of eight children. The precise whereabouts of what she witnessed are minimal; she never discussed the Armenian Genocide with anyone because it was too horrific. Her sister, Seranoosh "Arevalouys" (Kurkjian) Vartanian, spoke about what they experienced shortly after Kagazig's passing, allowing Kagazig's experience to be documented.

Kagazig was 12 years old when the Genocide began. The Turkish soldiers murdered most of her family and tried to take her as a child bride. She walked for months barefoot, and had many cuts and wounds on her feet; it was a miracle she survived. Her and her Seranoosh lived and worked in a factory for a couple years before going to live at an orphanage. Due to the horrific shock she witnessed from her family's murders, she never spoke of what happened for the rest of her life.

Several years later, when Kagazig was 19 and her sister, Seranoosh was 20, they met Sohig Vartanian at the orphanage. She traveled there in search of finding someone to marry her brother, Neghos Vartanian, and move to The United States. Sohig chose Seranoosh to be her brother's wife, and Seranoosh said she would only come if Sohig brought her sister, Kagazig, and their brother, Stephan, and found someone for both of them to marry. The only way Stephan was allowed to enter The United States was by changing his name from Stephan Kurkjian to Stephan Vartanian, to appear that he and Sohig were relatives. It was agreed, and they traveled to Ellis Island, New York.

Once they were allowed into The United States, Sohig, Seranoosh, Kagazig, and Stephan traveled from Ellis Island to Indian Orchard, Massachusetts where Kagazig met and married Mardiros Godoshian

Sohig then brought them to Pontiac, Michigan, where they were happily married for 61 years and had four children: Sema (Godoshian) Dakesian, twins Sally (Godoshian) Kabodian, and Sirouhi (Godoshian) Kemsuzian, and Michael Godoshian.

Stephan Kurkjian (Vartanian) married Ann Vartanian, and they had a daughter, Helene, but unfortunately, both Ann and Helene died. Stephan was devastated but found love again and married Caroline Vartanian; they lived the rest of their lives happily together.

Kagazig's story was shared by her daughter, Sally (Godoshian) Kabodian. She was a wonderful Armenian mother dedicated to her family. She had a lovely voice, loved reciting Armenian poetry, and was a member of the St. John's Armenian Church for 67 years, and she will always be remembered.

˄From Left: Kagazig (Kurkjian) Godoshian &
Stephan Kurkjian Vartanian

˄From Left: Seranoosh (Kurkjian) Vartanian &
Kagazig (Kurkjian) Godoshian

[54] Image provided by Sally (Godoshian) Kabodian
[55] Image provided by Sally (Godoshian) Kabodian

Giragos Kabadian

Giragos Kabadian was born on September 1st, 1895, in Keghi / Kakavaberd, Armenia, to Toros Kabadian and Mariam (Shemooian) Kabadian, who owned a beautiful farm and raised sheep. Giragos was a Keghitize, meaning he was an Armenian from Keghi.

His father sent his older brother to work in Branford, Canada, to send back earnings to his family. At the age of 18, Giragos was sent on the ship, La Touraine, to go to Ellis Island, New York, and arrived on October 27th, 1913.[56] He traveled to work in Branford, Canada, and his brother went home right before the Armenian Genocide began.

In Keghi, a young Turkish man worked on Giragos' family's farm for many years, and wanted to marry his sister, which his Father would not allow. When the Genocide began, the Turkish man came back to the farm and killed Giragos's entire family. Giragos cherished his marriage with Annig even more because he had no living family.

A year after Giragos and Annig married in Brantford, Canada, they had their eldest son, Hrog Kabodian in 1924. It is not known how some of their children's last names were changed from Kabadian to Kabodian.

[56] La Touraine, 27 October 1927; images, "Passenger Search," Statue of Liberty— Ellis Island Foundation https://heritage.statueofliberty.org/ship-details/czoxMToiTGEgVG91cmFpbmUiOw==/czoxMDoiMTkxMy0xMC0yNy17/czo0OiJzaGlwIjs=/czowOiIiOw==/czozOiI0OTAiOw: Accessed 9 October 2020.

Afterward, they traveled to Detroit, Michigan, and had their second son, Zorob Kabodian, in 1926. Soon after they moved to Pontiac, Michigan, Giragos worked for Wilson Foundry, and for General Motors; and their daughter, Nazeli "Hazel" Kabodian, was born in Pontiac in 1928. They had twin boys, Paramaz and Raffi, in 1931, who passed away after they were born. Their doctor told them having another child would help their grief, and Alice was born in 1937.

Giragos' life story was retold by his daughters, Nazeli "Hazel" Kabodian and Alice Kabodian. Giragos and Annig had a happy marriage and loved being a part of their Armenian community. Giragos passed away at the age of 80 in 1975 in Pontiac, Michigan.

57

⌃ Back from left: Annig Aprahamian Kabadian, &
Giragos Kabadian

Front from left: Nazeli "Hazel" Kabodian, Hrog
Kabodian, & Zorob Kabodian

⌃ The La Touraine   58

---

57 Image provided by Adam Asadoorian
58 La Touraine, 27 October 1927; images, "Passenger Search," Statue of Liberty— Ellis Island Foundation https://heritage.statueofliberty.org/ship-details/czoxMToiTGEgVG91cmFpbmUiOw==/czoxMDoiMTkxMy0xMC0yNy17/czo0OiJzaGlwIjs=/czowOiIiOw==/czozOiI0OTAiaiOw: Accessed 9 October 2020.

Annig (Aprahamian) Kabadian

Annig (Aprahamian) Kabadian was born on September 29th, 1905, in Kharpert / Harput Armenia, to Apraham and Siranoush (Kazanjian) Aprahamian. She was a Kharpertize; meaning she was an Armenian from Kharpert. Her infancy years are unknown because she was orphaned at a very young age due to the Armenian Genocide.

At the beginning of the Genocide, Annig was three years old, and her younger brother, Haroutun, was seven months old. Their parents took them to The German Missionary Orphanage, hoping to return once the Genocide passed but, unfortunately, they were both killed. Annig lived in The German Missionary Girls Orphanage, and Haroutun lived in The German Missionary Boys Orphanage. Since the Turkish soldiers burned all personal records, they did not know each other until several years later. It is believed that the orphanage received a note their parents gave the orphanage, which included their relation to one another.

The orphanages were very safe and took care of the orphans from the Genocide. Annig's role at the orphanage was to keep track of the pantry's inventory. Once the orphans turned 15, they had to live on their own. The orphans would stand in a designated section outside of the orphanage in hopes of work; people passing by knew that area meant they were orphans that needed work and would hire them to take care of their family's needs. When Annig was 15, she was chosen by a family who owned a grocery store, and she worked there and lived with them for a few years. The family was friendly, and they wanted Annig would marry their son, but instead, she decided to go to America. Annig and her brother kept in close contact since they were young, as they were each other's only living family. Haroutun was hesitant on Annig to go live in America but knew he had to support her.

Annig arranged to meet an Armenian man named Giragos Kabadian upon her arrival in America. She wanted to make sure he knew how to read and write in Armenian, so they wrote letters and got to know each other before meeting. She was 18 when she boarded the ship, The Constantinople, to go to The United States. The boat was very safe, and she traveled with friends; and on August 1st, 1923, she arrived on Ellis Island, New York.[59] Giragos was in Brantford, Canada, so she traveled by train to meet him at the Canadian train station, and they married several months later on March 29th, 1924, in Brantford.

Annig and Giragos had a happy marriage, had six children, and loved being a part of their Armenian community in Southeastern, Michigan, where they resided shortly after marriage. Annig passed away in 1991 at the age of 86 in Rochester Hills, Michigan.

Alice and Nazeli, who shared the stories and events about their parents and Uncle's survival, spoke about how Annig, Giragos,

---

[59] Aprahamian, Annig. 1 August 1923, Constantinople, age 22; stamped p.813, line 18 "Passenger Search," Statue of Liberty— Ellis Island Foundation https://heritage.statueofliberty.org/passenger-result: Accessed 9 October 2020

and Haroutun persevered and survived because of their love, kindness, wisdom, and strength.

⌃ From Left: Giragos Kabadian &
Annig (Aprahamian) Kabadian

⌃ The Constantinople   61

---

[60] Image provided by Adam Asadoorian
[61] Aprahamian, Annig. 1 August 1923, Constantinople, age 22; stamped p.813, line 18 "Passenger Search," Statue of Liberty— Ellis Island Foundation https://heritage.statueofliberty.org/passenger-result; Accessed 9 October 2020

Haroutun Terzian

Haroutun Terzian, Annig (Aprahamian) Kabadian's brother, was born in Kharpert / Harput Armenia, to Apraham and Siranoush (Kazanjian) Aprahamian. Haroutun was orphaned at seven months old and lived at The German Missionary Boys Orphanage his entire childhood as a result of the Armenian Genocide. He never went by the last name of Aprahamian, and was 14 when he left The German Missionary Boys Orphanage and to become a tailor's apprentice. He eventually owned a tailor's shop, Arto's Menswear, which was successful. He married Verkeen (Basmadjian) and took her Step-Fathers name, Terzian, because his wife's family wanted their last name to carry onto the next generation.

They had four children: Maritza (Terzian) Panossian, Briske (Terzian) Mampourian, Hampartsoum "Hampy" Terzian, and Yester (Terzian) Manankichian. Haroutun eventually owned a manufacturing company with his son Hampartsoum called Hampy's Menswear. Haroutun and Verkeen were Christian, and they would always share their wealth and food with others, especially their employees. He was blessed with a happy marriage, family with Verkeen, and a very successful career. Haroutun died in 1970 in Beirut, Lebanon. Their son, Hampartsoum resides in Beirut, Lebanon, along with his family, where he continued running his Father's company until they sold their business.

Alice and Nazeli spoke fondly about their parents, Annig and Giragos, and their Uncle Haroutun. They spoke when in 1956, Annig reunited with Haroutun in Beirut. Annig, Giragos, Alice and Nazeli visited Haroutun and his family for an entire summer in Beirut, Lebanon. It was a wonderful reunion, and they stayed at their Uncle's beautiful home on the Mediterranean Sea. Nazeli and Alice said it was one of the best times of their lives.

Back from left: Maritza (Terzian) Panossian & Antranik Panossian
Front from left: Verkeen (Basmadjian) Terzian, Briske (Terzian) Mampourian, Hampartsoum Terzian, Yester (Terzian) Manankichian, & Haroutun Terzian

---

62 Image provided by Adam Asadoorian

Marguerite "Margaret" (Krechchin) Masropian

Marguerite "Margaret" (Krechchin) Masropian was born in 1906 in Van, Armenia. She lived near Mt. Ararat with her loving family; and she was incredibly close to her Mother and sisters. The beginning of the Armenian Genocide caused havoc on Armenians in Van; due to the persecution, she was very fearful for her families' lives.

During the Genocide, she received a letter from her friend, Markar Masropian, who knew of the Krechchin family. In the letter, he wrote he was looking for a bride from Armenia to come to Canada, and marry his brother, David Masropian. Markar and David Masropian immigrated to Canada from Armenia for work, before the Genocide. Marguerite's family pleaded with her to leave and go to Canada so she could survive. At the age of 19, in 1924, she traveled to Canada; due to the threat Armenians faced from the Genocide, Marguerite could only travel with valuables sewn in her coat's hems. It broke her heart she was never reunited with her family because of the Genocide.

Shortly after arriving in Canada, David and Marguerite were married in Guelph, Ontario, and then they moved to Windsor, Ontario. David worked in a rubber factory and made shoes before working for The Ford Motor Company. Marguerite worked for AJ Gervais Furrier; she was also an excellent seamstress who created beautiful clothes. Marguerite and David had three children: Louise

Masropian (Davidian), Mae Masropian, and Anne (Masropian) Kabodian. Anne was a child prodigy violinist and would do concerts and solos with orchestras in Windsor and Toronto, Canada. David and Marguerite were also very close to David's brother, Markar, because they were the only family they had in Canada. Markar lived in Windsor, Ontario, with his wife, Arpeneg Masropian, who was also from Armenia with their children.

Marguerite and David lived a happy life together until David's passing in 1965, at the age of 70; and Marguerite died in 1980, at the age of 74, in Windsor Ontario. Margaret and David were devote Armenians and attended St. John's Anglican Church in Windsor, Ontario.

Laurie (Kabodian) Jackson, Marguerite's granddaughter, retold her story. She spoke about how Marguerite continued her Armenian family legacy, and recalled how her Grandmother and her late sister, Janice Kabodian, loved to garden together in the summer. Marguerite's granddaughter, Denise (Davidian) King, remembered her Grandmother as an excellent cook who also loved to garden.

《 Back from left:
David Masropian,
Louise (Masropian)
Davidian, & Marguerite
"Margaret" (Krechchin)
Masropian

Front from left: Mae
Masropian & Anne
(Masropian) Kabodian

⌃ Fourth row from left: Hrog Kabodian, Anne (Masropian) Kabodian,
Denise (Davidian) King, & Ralph Davidian
Third row from left: Nazeli Kabadian, Annig (Aprahamian) Kabadian,
Marguerite "Margaret" (Krechchin) Masropian, Louise (Masropian)
Davidian, Alice (Kabodian) Asadoorian, Janice Kabadian,
& Zorob Kabodian
Second row from left: Mae Masropian, Giragos Kabadian,
& David Masropian,
First row: Cathy (Davidian) Hendel

63 Image provided by Laurie (Kabodian) Jackson
64 Image provided by Laurie (Jackson) Kabodian

Armenag Klavanian

Armenag Klavanian was born in 1895 in Sebastia, "Sivas" Turkey. In 1914, a year before the Armenian Genocide, his Father sent him to work in The United States. When the Genocide began in 1915, Armenag returned to be a soldier in the General Andranik Regime.

Upon his arrival in Armenia, he went to his home village and was informed that his entire family (his six siblings, parents, cousins, aunts, uncles and grandparents) were murdered by the Turkish soldiers. One of his sisters killed herself to avoid rape by throwing herself into a river.

In the aftermath of the Genocide, Armenag went back to The United States and then moved to Canada to be with his brother-in-law, Garabed Mooradian, a fellow Armenian soldier who survived the Genocide. Garabed's wife, Maritza, was presumed dead from the Genocide; but in 1920, she was found alive and traveled to Canada and was reunited with her husband and brother. Unfortunately, their one-year-old daughter died from starvation in the Genocide during The Death March.

Shortly after Maritza immigrated to Canada, she and Armenag worked together to immigrate her friend, Zevart (Zarkaryan) Klavanian, to The United States to marry Armenag, who had recently relocated to Detroit, Michigan, to work for The Ford Motor Company. They were married in 1930 and had four children: Vartoui (Klavanian) Smith, Aghavni Klavanian (who passed away as an infant), Dicran Klavanian, and Aghavni "Agnes" (Klavanian) Markarian.

Armenag and Zevart were married for 40 years in Detroit until Zevart passed away in 1951, and Armenag passed away in 1976. Aghavni married Nerses Markarian in 1958, and had two sons, Andrew "Andy" Markarian and Arthur "Art" Markarian. Armenag's story was told by his youngest daughter, Aghavni (Klavanian) Markarian, who remembered him as a kind person, and he loved to read.

A From Left: Zevart (Zarkaryan) Klavanian, & Armenag Klavanian

A From Left: Aghavni (Klavanian) Markarian, Armenag Klavanian, Dicran Klavanian, & Zevart (Zarkaryan) Klavanian

[65] Image provided by Aghavni (Klavanian) Markarian
[66] Image provided by Aghavni (Klavanian) Markarian

Rose (Aprahamian / Mooradian) Sherinian

Rose (Aprahamian Mooradian) Sherinian's story was told by her niece, Barbara (Dourjalian) Widener. Rose was born on November 11th, 1911, in Samsun, Turkey, on the Black Sea's coast, in the Mediterranean. Her Father, Sirigan Aprahamian, owned a barbershop, and was a young widow; his wife passed away when Rose was very young. Sirigan remarried to Ardem Serijanian in 1913, and raised Rose as her own. Sirigan and Ardem had two daughters: Mary (Aprahamian) Minoogian and Alice (Aprahamian) Gedikian. Ardem was a school teacher who graduated from Marsivan College and was well respected.

In June 1915, right before the Armenian Genocide began, the Turkish soldiers came into Samsun to gather all the Armenian men and to enlist in the Turkish Army. Her Mother and Father were informed that if they converted to Islam, Sirigan would not have to enlist. However, because they were devout Christian Armenians, they would not consider changing their religion. The last time Rose saw her Father was when he was being taken by the Turkish soldiers and was killed.

Afterwards, her Mother, Ardem, was suddenly left alone to care for three girls at the beginning of a Genocide. For her daughters to survive, she temporarily give her children to live with three different Grecians families. Rose's six month old sister, Mary, went to live with a Grecian family on a farm. Rose and her two year old sister, Alice, went to separate Grecian families. These families took great care of the girls, and were very kind people; and Ardem would occasionally safely visit.

Soon afterward, the Samsun town caller announced that they would hang anyone hiding Armenians. Upon hearing this, her Mother gathered her three daughters out of fear that the Grecian families would be killed. A Grecian man helped them get to a safe government building. There, the mayor of Samsun spared them because they were women and children. They then had to live in a Church's basement for a couple of years because the Turkish soldiers took their home. The living conditions were very poor; they were constantly sick because of the freezing basement temperature; they also had lice, sores, were dirty, and had limited amounts of clothing and food. Every night they would fall asleep to the noise of bombings in the distance. Unfortunately, this was something that Rose carried with her throughout the rest of her life; she could never forget the sounds of the Genocide.

Through The American Red Cross, Ardem was able to get in contact with her sister, Aznive (Serijanian) Serunian, and her brother-in-law, Moses Serunian, who lived in The United States, and offered their monetary assistance so they could immigrate there. Ardem and her daughters then traveled to Carsamba, Turkey, where they stayed for a couple of months. In August 1920, they boarded onto a ship named The Gul Djemal and set sail.[67] While they were in the Atlantic Ocean, many people got sick and died, and it was a frightful ordeal.

When Rose was eight, Alice was five, and Mary was four years old, they arrived to Ellis Island, New York, on October, 31st, 1920. Aznive and Moses Serunian greeted Ardem and her girls and brought them to their house in Portland, Maine, where they lived there for a few years. Rose recalled loving her time in Portland; she was thankful she was never afraid or hungry.

A couple of years later, in Portland, Ardem was set up with Pilos Mooradian. They fell in love and got married in 1922 in Portland, Maine, and had two children, Stephen Mooradian and Aznive "Agnes" (Mooradian) Dourjalian.

When Rose was 20, she met and married, Hess Sherinian, in Portland, Maine before moving together to Detroit, Michigan. Ironically, Rose and Hess knew each other when they were young; Hess would go to The American Red Cross for soup and bring it to her family when they lived in the Church's basement. Rose and Hess settled in Detroit, Michigan, and two had children, Donald Sherinian and Robert Sherinian.

Ardem and Pilos Mooradian had a very happy marriage; they both died in their 80s in California.

---

[67] Gul Djemal, 31 October 1920; images, "Passenger Search," Statue of Liberty— Ellis Island Foundation. Accessed on 10.9.2020. Retrieved from: (https://heritage.statueofliberty.org/ship-details/czoxMDoiR3VsIERqZW1hbCI7/czoxMDoiMTkyMC0xMC0zMSI7/czo4OiJtYW5pZmVzdCI7/czowOiIiOw==/czo1OiIyMTQxMCI7

Rose and Hess Sherinian lived a good life together until Hess passed away in 1988; Rose lived well until the age of 89 and passed away on March 27th, 2000.

From Left: Rose (Aprahamian) Sherinian, & Sirigan Aprahamian [68]

The Gul Djemal [69]

[68] Image provided by Barbara (Dourjalian) Widener
[69] Gul Djemal, 31 October 1920; images, "Passenger Search," Statue of Liberty— Ellis Island Foundation. Accessed on 10.9.2020. Retrieved from: (https://heritage.statueofliberty.org/ship-details/czoxMDoiR3VsIERqZW1hbCI7/czoxMDoiMTkyMC0xMC0zMSI7/czo4OiJtYW5pZmVzdCI7/czowOiIiOw==/czo1OilyMTQxMCI7

Hovhaness Dourjalian

Hovhaness Dourjalian's story was retold by his granddaughter, Barbara (Dourjalian) Widener. Hovhaness was born in 1881 in Yozgat, Turkey. At the age of 26, in 1907, Hovhaness, his parents, and brother traveled to The United States, and eventually became citizens in 1914. Shortly afterwards, he traveled back to Turkey for business, and while he traveled in Turkey, his brother and father remained in The United States. Upon his arrival to Turkey, the Armenian Genocide had begun and he was detained and jailed by the Turkish soldiers.

He insisted to the Turkish soldiers that he was an American citizen, and after two days, was advised that he would be allowed to return to The United States, and was released. But when he tried to leave Turkey again, the Turkish Police would not approve, and they beat and robbed him. Afterward, he fled Istanbul, Turkey, and walked to the American Consul in Aleppo. There, he contacted his father and brother who sent him $4,000 to survive.

Hovhaness stayed in Aleppo for a few years, concealing himself to survive and lived in poverty. During his time there, he met his wife Nevart (Dilan) and had two children, Woodrow Dourjalian and Virginia Dourjalian.

When the Genocide was over, he traveled back to The United States with his family on the ship, The S.S Rotterdam. [70]

---

[70] Douroujalian, Woodrow. 30 May 1920. S.S. Rotterdam stamped p. 279, line 23. "Passenger Search," Statue of Liberty— Ellis Island Foundation. Accessed on 10.9.2020. Retrieved from: https://heritage.statueofliberty.org/passenger-details/czoxMjoiNjA0NDc3MDcwMDYyIjs=/czo5OiJwYXNzZW5nZXXIiOw:

Unfortunately, Virginia died of dehydration on the boat and had to hide their deceased daughter when they disembarked to give her a proper burial on land. Once they arrived at Ellis Island, New York, they went to Detroit, Michigan, where they had two more children, Edward and Noubar. They lived the rest of their lives together in the Detroit until Hovhaness died at 56.

[71]

Hovhaness Dourjalian

[72]

The S.S. Rotterdam

[71] Image provided by Barbara (Dourjalian) Widener
[72] The Statue of Liberty—Ellis Island Foundation, Inc S.S. Rotterdam image. Accessed on 1.3.2021. Retrieved from: https://heritage.statueofliberty.org/ship-details/czo5OiJSb3R0ZXJkYW0iOw==/czoxMDoiMTk0OS0wMS0wMSI7/czo0OiJzaGlwIjs=/czowOiIiOw==/czozOiIxODgiOw==

Stephan Karakashian

Stephan "Steve" Karakashian was born in 1905 in Evereg, Turkey, and was the middle child of five children. When the Armenian Genocide began, he was ten years old; the Genocide caused his family to be displaced. As a result, his two younger twin sisters died, and he was placed in an orphanage full of other Armenian children orphaned at the hands of the Ottoman Empire.

Stephan was an extremely resourceful child. At night, he would crawl over the orphanage fence and sell eggs to the Turkish soldiers. From his earnings, he would then get food and bring it to the fellow Armenian orphans. The Turkish soldiers only bought the eggs because they assumed he was Turkish. Stephan saved some gold coins from his earnings and was able to locate the whereabouts of his brother and Father. Unfortunately, both of them were in one of the Armenian concentration camps controlled by Turkish soldiers. Utilizing his resourcefulness, Stephan bribed the soldiers with the gold he had accumulated to free his brother and Father. It was a miracle they survived because the very next morning, all the Armenians at the concentration camp were ordered into the desert, where they were shot and killed. His resourcefulness saved both his brother's and Father's lives.

Eventually, Stephan earned enough money and solely ventured off to the island of Cyprus. He traveled to Cairo, Egypt, and then to Cuba, where he stayed for about a year. During that time, he saved up money by shoe shinning to immigrate to The United States. Once Stephan gathered his earned funds, he paid someone to hide him in the freighter's boiler room. There were many other young adults in there with him; they were all so hot down there from the boilers, and he did not know if he would survive.

He survived the journey and finally arrived in Mobile, Alabama, where he was taken to a hotel. He was instructed to stay put while the soldiers went to get the authorities. Stephan realized what was about to ensure and escaped with a small bag of belongings because he knew they would send him back to Cuba, so he ran to a nearby train station and boarded onto a train. All he had in order to communicate with anyone was a piece of paper in his pocket with his Uncle from Chicago, Illinois address, written in English. Luckily, he showed it to someone who directed him to get onto the right train and traveled from Alabama to Chicago.

Once he arrived in Chicago, he somehow found his way to his Uncle's street. It is unknown how he made it because he did not speak any English and had no idea exactly where he was going. When he arrived at his Uncle's, there was no one at the house because his Uncle was at work, so Stephan waited outside for the whole day until his Uncle came home.

Stephan stayed in Chicago with his Uncle for a year and then moved to Detroit. Some Armenians in the Metro Detroit Area helped him get a factory job at Ford Motor Company at the Highland Park Plant. Stephan did not like working at the factory. Stephan mistook the red tobacco spit as blood and thought they had tuberculosis; he did not realize they were all chewing tobacco. While Stephan worked at the Ford Plant, he would send money back to his family. Eventually, his parents, sister, and brother immigrated to The United States, where they were reunited.

After leaving Ford Motor Company, Stephan got a job at a dry cleaner though another Armenian connection. He worked as an unpaid apprentice for a few months, and then once he gained experience and mastered the skill, he was well paid, and he thoroughly enjoyed this line of work.

Stephan met his wife, Sevart (Stamboulian) Karakashian, through a Church event in Detroit, Michigan. Sevart was an Armenian born in The United States, and they got married in 1938. They lived a loving life together and had three children, Jack Karakashian, Robert "Bobby" Karakashian, and Mary Ann (Karakashian) Artinian.

Stephan Karakashian passed away at the age of 88 in 1993. His son, Robert Karakashian, who told his Father's story, described him as an incredibly courageous person. Stephan's heroic acts were so noble that Armenian survivors who immigrated to Detroit spoke highly of Stephan's because they survived off of the food he gave them when they were children in the orphanage at the beginning of the Armenian Genocide.

73

From Left: Jack Karakashian, Stephan Karakashian, &
Robert "Bobby" Karakashian

73 Image provided by Denise (Dourjalian) Karakashian

Zabel (Lachinian) Soultanian

Zabel (Lachinian) Soultanian was born on September 2nd, 1907, in Konya, Turkey, to Levon and Gulizar (Shimsherian) Lachinian. She was the middle child of four siblings: Arshalous, Mgerdich, Sirar, and Hagop Lachinian.

Zabel was eight years old when the Armenian Genocide began in 1915. Her Father, Levon, and her 12 year old brother, Mgerdich, were murdered by the Turkish soldiers. When deportation orders came for the remainder of her family, they traveled in a horse-drawn wagon to the concentration camp, Deir ez-Zor, in the middle of the Syrian Desert. An unknown event transpired, and their wagon and belongings were stolen along the way and Zabel's two Uncles were never seen again. Zabel's Mother, Aunt, and sisters had to travel the remainder of the journey by foot to arrive to the Deir ez-Zor concentration camp.

After some time at Deir ez-Zor, her family was taken to an American Protestant orphanage where her Mother, Gulizar, and Aunt Nazen (Shimsherian) Papazian worked as cooks to spare their children from being separated. While at the orphanage, Zabel and her older sister, Arshalous (Lachinian) Sarafian, learned to speak English from The American Relief workers. Shortly after that, Zabel and her family were transported to Zahlé, Lebanon.

A few years later, in 1925, Zabel met her future husband, Tavit Soultanian who was from Evereg, Turkey. He was the youngest of five brothers: Harutoun, Armenag, Garabed, and Hagop Soultanian. During WWI, Tavit was recruited to go to Beirut to fight Turkey. While he was in Beirut, he visited Zahlé, where he met, Zabel and fell in love.

Zabel and Tavit got married shortly after meeting and had two children, Sarkis Soultanian and Alice (Soultanian) Zallakian. Unfortunately, Tavit contracted pneumonia and died at 32 years old. Zabel left Zhalé with her children, her mother, and her siblings to settle in Beirut. They lived there for many years, while Zabel worked as a tailor/seamstress.

Many years later, Sarkis immigrated to Michigan in the early 1950s to live and work with his Uncle, Armenag. Zabel and left Beirut in 1956, arrived in New York and then traveled to Michigan to be with her family.

Zabel never remarried, and she lived a full and happy life with her children and five grandchildren. Zabel passed away on November 7th, 1997, at the age of 90 years old. She is remembered for her strong faith, courage, and determination in giving her children a better life.

Zabel's story was shared by her daughter, Alice (Soultanian) Zallakian, and grandchildren: Anne Marie (Zallakian) Ameriguian, and Michael "Raffi" Zallakian.

74

Zabel (Lachinian) Soultanian

[74] Image provided by Anne Marie (Zallakian) Ameriguian, M.D.

Hampartzoum Zallakian

Hampartzoum Zallakian was born in 1900 in Sebastia/ Sivas, Turkey, to Stepan and Aghavni Zallakian. Hampartzoum was 15 when the Genocide began. He, his Mother Aghavni, and his three sisters (Rebekah, Osanna, and Mariam Zallakian) survived the Armenian Genocide, but his Father, Stepan, was killed. Hampartzoum, was determined to escape Sebastia / Sivas, Turkey, in the hope of safety for him and his family and began a treacherous journey on foot to Istanbul, Turkey.

With only the clothes on his back, Hampartzoum walked through Turkish land to Istanbul, Turkey. He was frequently stopped along the way by Turkish soldiers; because he spoke Turkish, they assumed he was Turkish and spared his life. During this terrifying journey, he was beaten and left without shoes; but he completed the remainder of his pilgrimage to Istanbul.

Once Hampartzoum arrived in Constantinople/Istanbul, he found a job working with a merchant who would send him to Marseille, France, to trade his goods. As the years went by, the merchant asked Hampartzoum to join him in partnership, but his goal was to leave Turkey; he used his earnings to bring his sisters and mother to Istanbul.

Hamparetzoum met Chenorik (Hembelian) through his boss, and they had an arranged marriage in 1922. Shortly afterward, they moved to Marseille, France, with Hampartzoum's Mother and sisters. Hampartzoum and Chenorik had three children: George, Vehanoush "Josephine" Zallakian, and Anahid (Zallakian) Kazanjian.   Soon after WWII, George immigrated to The United States and gained employment used his earnings to bring his parents and sisters to Detroit, Michigan. Hampartzoum and Chenorik lived a good life together with their family until Hampartzoum passed away in 1975 at 75. His strength, survival, and perseverance will always be honored.

Hampartzoum's story was shared by his grandchildren: Anne Marie (Zallakian) Ameriguian, and Michael "Raffi" Zallakian.

Hampartzoum Zallakian

75 Image provided by Anahid (Zallakian) Kazanjia

Chenorik (Hembelian) Zallakian

Chenorik (Hembelian) Zallakian was an Armenian Genocide survivor who carried the horrific incidents from the Genocide with her throughout her life. Her parents, Lousanoush and Hagop Hembelian, had two daughters, and one of them was named Chenorik.

Chenorik was born in 1907, in the village of Sebinkarahisar, Turkey. The Turkish soldiers killed her Father during the Shabin-Karahisar Uprising, and Chenorik never spoke of her memories of the Genocide, as this always brought her to tears.

Soon after the Shabin-Karahisar Uprising occurred, a Turkish man came to the Hembelian home with the specific intention of taking Chenorik to marry his son. Chenorik was not home, but her beautiful, younger sister was there, and instead, she was forcefully taken by the Turkish soldier. Chenorik's sister was kidnapped and forced to marry the Turkish soldier. Chenorik and her mother were devastated by this event and prayed she would safely return. No one knows what happened to her sister; her sister's horrific loss remained in Chenorik's heart until her death.

A few years later, Chenorik and Hampartzoum were married in an arranged marriage. Their lives were blessed with children, grandchildren, and great-grandchildren. They lived happy, fulfilling lives, and Chenorik passed at the age of 91 in 1998, and is with her sister in heaven.

Zabel's story was shared by her grandchildren: Anne Marie (Zallakian) Ameriguian, and Michael "Raffi" Zallakian.

From Left: Hampartzoum Zallakian &
Chenorik (Hembelian) Zallakian

---

[76] Image provided by Anne Marie (Zallakian) Ameriguian, M.D.

Epilogue

Armenians existence has remained in peril even after the Armenian Genocide and the Istanbul Pogrom. More specifically, the events that occurred in 2020 in The Republic of Artsakh served as a horrific reminder of the Armenian Genocide.

Armenia and Azerbaijan have had a long history of conflict regarding who will live on a portion of land, known to Armenia, as The Republic of Artsakh, and known to Azerbaijan as Nagorno-Karabakh.[77] This land was originally inhabited by Armenians in the early 5th Century B.C...[78] In July 2020, Armenia experienced a present-day ethnic cleansing[79] when Azerbaijan threatened to blow up Armenia's nuclear power plant.[80]

The term ethnic cleansing refers to the violent organized attempt to completely remove all members from a country or area.[81] When Azerbaijan instigated the conflict in July, and Turkey then funded their military aid, held Armenian medical equipment hostage,[82] and hired Syrian men to fight for them for compensation.[83]

[77] Stronski, Paul. Carnegie Endowment for International Peace. *Behind the Flare-Up Along Armenia-Azerbaijan Border.* Retrieved on 12.29.2020. Accessed from: https://carnegieendowment.org/2020/07/22/behind-flare-up-along-armenia-azerbaijan-border-pub-82345
[78] Office of Nagorno Karabakh Republic. *Nagorno Karabakh (Artsakh): Historical And Geographical Perspectives.* Retrieved on 12.29.2020. Accessed from: http://www.nkrusa.org/country_profile/history.shtml
[79] Mark, Nicole. The Observer. *The Armenian Genocide of 2020: The Fight for Indigenous Armenian Land.* 15 November 2020. Retrieved on 12.29.2020. Accessed from: https://fordhamobserver.com/52231/opinions/the-armenian-genocide-of-2020-the-fight-for-indigenous-armenian-land/
[80] Stronski, Paul. Carnegie Endowment for International Peace. *Behind the Flare-Up Along Armenia-Azerbaijan Border.* Retrieved on 12.29.2020. Accessed from: https://carnegieendowment.org/2020/07/22/behind-flare-up-along-armenia-azerbaijan-border-pub-82345
[81] Cambridge Dictionary. Ethnic cleansing. Retrieved on 12.29.2020. Accessed from: https://dictionary.cambridge.org/us/dictionary/english/ethnic-cleansing 12.30.2020.
[82] Global Awareness Initiative. *Global Awareness Initiative Reports Turkey Blocked 100 Tons of Humanitarian Aid to Armenia.* 15 October 2020. Retrieved on 12.29.2020. Accessed from: https://www.prnewswire.com/news-releases/global-awareness-initiative-reports-turkey-blocked-100-tons-of-humanitarian-aid-to-armenia-301153765.html
[83] Abdulrahim, Raja. The Wall Street Journal. *Turkish-Backed Syrian Fighters Join Armenian-Azeri Conflict.* 14 October 2020. Retrieved on 12.29.2020. Accessed from: https://www.wsj.com/articles/turkish-backed-syrian-fighters-join-armenian-azeri-conflict-11602625885

Turkey and Azerbaijan denied that their actions were an ethnic cleansing falsely blamed Armenia.[84]

On November 11th, 2020 EST; the Prime Minister of Armenia and the President of Artsakh, signed the land of Artsakh over to Azerbaijan to avoid further destruction after Turkey and Azerbaijan took control of Shushi; one of the largest cities in Artsakh.[85] As a result of this present-day ethnic cleaning towards Armenia,[86] 70,000 Armenians were displaced due to being forced to flee their homeland in Artsakh. About 2,500 Armenian military soldiers were killed, and hundreds of Armenian civilians were injured.[87] This conflict was also carried out through the use of Azerbaijan military drones, which severely impacted the overall outcome.[88]

All Armenians want to live peacefully, but most importantly – survive.

[84] Gulesserian, Lisa and David L. Phillips. The Institute for the Study of Human Rights. *THE MEDIA WAR BY AZERBAIJAN AND TURKEY AGAINST ARMENIA AND NAGORNO-KARABAKH. 21 OCTOBER 2020.* Retrieved on 12.29.2020. Accessed from: https://www.humanrightscolumbia.org/news/media-war-azerbaijan-and-turkey-against-armenia-and-nagorno-karabakh
[85] The Armenian Weekly. Pashinyan, Aliyev and Putin sign agreement to end Karabakh War. November 2020. Retrieved on 12.29.2020. https://armenianweekly.com/2020/11/09/pashinyan-aliyev-and-putin-sign-agreement-to-end-karabakh-war/
[86] Mark, Nicole. The Observer. *The Armenian Genocide of 2020: The Fight for Indigenous Armenian Land.* 15 November 2020. Retrieved on 12.29.2020. Accessed from: https://fordhamobserver.com/52231/opinions/the-armenian-genocide-of-2020-the-fight-for-indigenous-armenian-land/
[87] France-Presse, Agence. The Guardian. *Half of Nagorno-Karabakh population displaced by Armenia and Azerbaijan clashes.* 7 October 2020. Retrieved on 12.29.2020. Accessed from: https://www.theguardian.com/world/2020/oct/08/half-of-nagorno-karabakh-population-displaced-by-armenia-and-azerbaijan-clashes
[88] Hambling, David. The 'Magic Bullet' Drones Behind Azerbaijan's Victory Over Armenia. 10 November 2020. Retrieved on 12.29.2020. Accessed from: https://www.forbes.com/sites/davidhambling/2020/11/10/the-magic-bullet-drones-behind--azerbaijans-victory-over-armenia/?sh=381a471b5e57

Index

About the Author

Ariana Anoush Kabodian was raised in Novi, Michigan where she currently resides. She attended Mercy High School and received her B.S. in Sustainable Business from Aquinas College, where she played on the Women's Collegiate Tennis Team. Ariana began her career working for Scripps Networks Interactive as part of the HGTV/DIY Ad Sales Marketing team, and currently works for a company as a Digital Account Manager. She is also nearing completion of her M.B.A., with a duel concentration in Entrepreneurship/Innovation, and Management, from Wayne State University. She is also an artist and designed this books illustrations.

[89]

Personal Photos

《 From Left: Meliné (Dilan) Artar, Belinda (Ameriguian) Kabodian, Ariana Kabodian, & Shoushan (Artar) Ameriguian

From Left: 》 Meliné (Dilan) Artar and Margaux Meliné Kabodian, whom her middle name is named after

《 Front from Left: Meliné Nichols, Meliné (Dilan) Artar, Robert Nichols, & Mesiya Artar

Back from Left: Belinda (Ameriguian) Kabodian, Linda Markarian, Brenda (Markarian) Barsoumian, Edward Markarian, & Thomas Markarian

90 Images provided by Belinda (Ameriguian) Kabodian
91 Images provided by Belinda (Ameriguian) Kabodian
92 Images provided by Belinda (Ameriguian) Kabodian

《 From Left: Meliné (Dilan) Artar & Ariana Kabodian

From Left: 》 Shoushan (Artar) Ameriguian, Ramela (Nushanian) Carman, (back) Belinda (Ameriguian) Kabodian & Ariana Kabodian

《 From Left: Seranoosh (Kurkjian) Vartanian & Ariana Kabodian

---

[93] Images provided by Belinda (Ameriguian) Kabodian
[94] Images provided by Armen Kabodian
[95] Images provided by Armen Kabodian

96

⌃ From Left: Armen Kabodian, Giragos
Kabadian & Aram Kabodian

97

⌃ From Left: Mardiros Godoshian, Kagazig (Kurkjian)
Godoshian, Sally (Godoshian) Kabodian, Zorob
Kabodian, Annig (Aprahamian) Kabadian,
& Giragos Kabadian